This Book Belongs To:

Stephen Curry

A Boy Who Became A Star

By

Stephen Herman

Stephen Curry: A Boy Who Became A Star.

ISBN: 978-1-948040-00-6

First Edition: September 2017
10 9 8 7 6 5 4 3 2 1

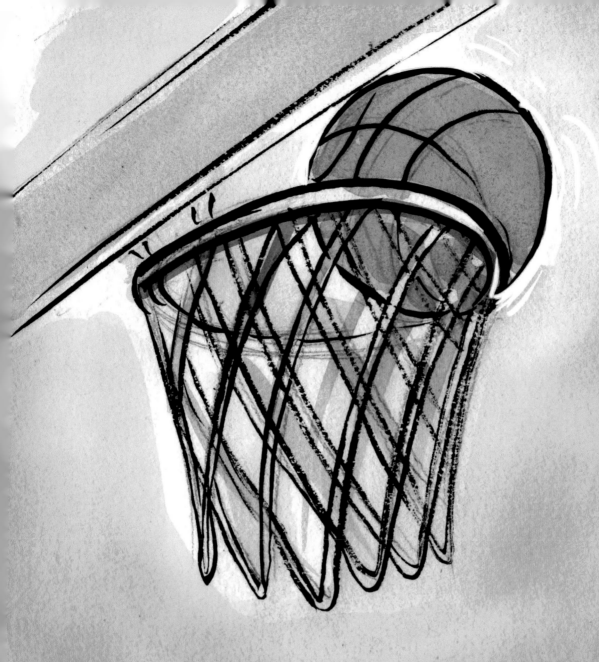

When Stephen was a child, he was much like me and you,
Dreaming of what he'd become and all the things he'd do.

"I wonder what I'll be," he thought, "when I am grown someday? I think I'll be just like my dad and play for the NBA!"

So Stephen drilled on skills, and he learned to play the game,
Someday when I am grown," he said, "folks will know my name!"

Stephen practiced every day, so he could reach his dream;
Eventually, his work paid off, and Stephen made the team!

Sometimes when Stephen had the ball and gave it his best shot,
Stephen missed – But did he quit? -- ABSOLUTELY NOT!

Stephen kept on playing, though he messed up now and then,
For when you want to be a star, you always try again.

Stephen's dedication and hard work are the reason
That Stephen led his team to an undefeated season.

Then Stephen went to Davidson to play college basketball,
But people doubted he could do it – they said he was too small.

But Stephen smiled and then replied, "Just you wait and see – You'll be surprised to realize, there's so much more to me.

"You can't see my heart by just looking with your eyes;
You don't see the best of me, if you just see my size."

Then Stephen led his school to where they'd never been before –
The NCAA tournament where they made the Final Four!

"Hip hip hurray!" the people say, "would you look at him?
He can score from middle court and from underneath the rim!"

Then Stephen jumped for joy for his childhood dream came true
When the Warriors of Golden State said, "Stephen, we want YOU!"

He'd followed in his father's steps up to the NBA,
For he had held onto his dream and not let it slip away.

Then Stephen suffered injuries, and folks feared he was through,
But Stephen healed and rallied back, 'cause that's what winners do!

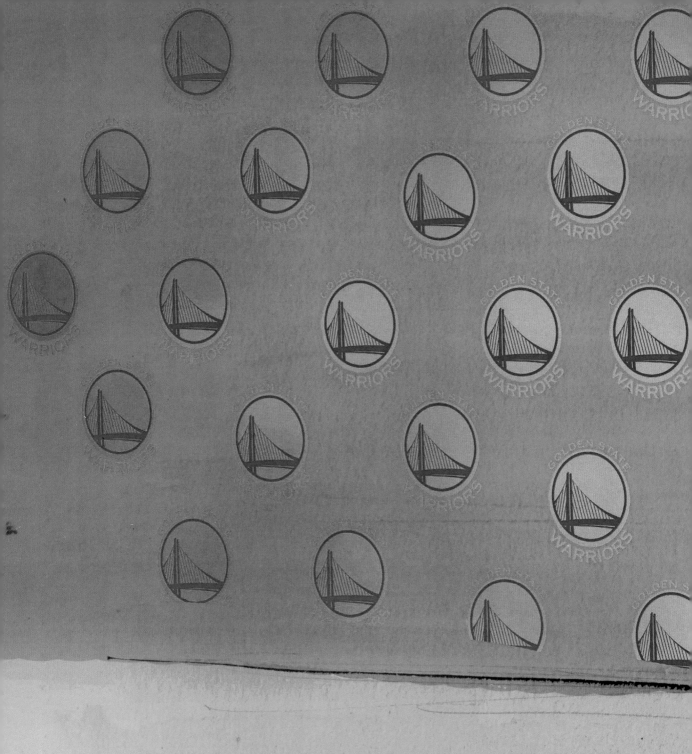

"But understand," he tells his fans, "how this all came to be" --
"I can do all things," he says, "through Christ Who strengthens me."

Made in the USA
Las Vegas, NV
30 January 2023

66474317R00031

ISBN 9781948040006

90000

9 781948 040006